When Chronic Pain and Illness Take Everything Away: How to Mourn Our Losses

Chronic Pain and the Christian Life Series

ESTHER SMITH

D1409889

When Chronic Pain and Illness Take Everything Away: How to Mourn Our Losses

© 2016 Esther Smith, First Edition

All rights reserved. No part of this book may be reproduced in any form or by any electronic or mechanical means – except in the case of brief quotations embodied in articles or reviews – without written permission from this publisher.

Unless otherwise noted, Scripture quotations are taken from the HOLY BIBLE, NEW INTERNATIONAL VERSION ®, NIV ® Copyright © 1973, 1979, 1984, 2011, by Biblica, Inc.™ Used by permission. All rights reserved.

Visit the author's website at lifeinslowmotionblog.com.

Contents

CHAPTER 1

The Things We Have Lost

I grew up in the outdoors. My family lived on a six-acre plot of land where my parents built their own house from the ground up. Our neighbor's property surrounded us, and all told, I had many miles of woods and fields, marshes and trails to roam about alone or with my friends. For hours of the day I would run and explore and simply be in the woods. I would look for animal tracks, attempt to garden, and read in the shade of my favorite trees until my mom rang the bell that signaled me home.

I guess you could say the wilderness has always been my place of comfort and safety. In the woods, I stalked butterflies, wasps, and grasshoppers, adding only the finest specimens to my growing collection. In the woods, I picked through acres of thorny black raspberry bushes until the huge metal bowl overflowed. I would come home tired and covered in red welts from the briars, but without a care in the world. These outdoor adventures I created were just what my 10-year-old self needed to be happy and content.

The woods never stopped calling my name. Throughout my middle school and high school years, I remember camping and biking trips with my youth group and kayaking and canoeing adventures with my family. Then in college, I became involved in an outdoor adventure program on our campus. Here I learned to backpack through the wilderness with a heavy pack on my hips. Here I learned to rock climb and lead groups on ropes course elements. For several summers, I worked as a ropes course facilitator, leading groups through games, initiatives, and high and low ropes course activities. I loved the active nature of this work where every day I played, laughed, and worked hard in the outdoors.

Immediately following college, I found work as an adventure based counseling assistant at a treatment facility for adjudicated youth. Once again, I played on ropes courses, practiced my rock climbing, and led youth through outdoor adventures for my job. Life was good. It felt like I was made for work such as this.

Perhaps more than anything else, memories of my years outside remind me how much chronic pain has changed me. I don't think it would be possible for me to set foot on a ropes course without bursting into tears at the stark reminder that I am not the same person I used to be. Just thinking about these wooded places that used to feel like home brings tears to my eyes, as I remember all I cannot do.

No longer can I run. No longer can I stand on my feet for hours at a time. No longer can I do any kind of physical work or play. No longer. These things I loved, these favorite parts of my childhood, teenage, and college years have all been taken away. And I won't be getting them back. I am not the same person I used to be, and some days I am not sure how to deal with that fact.

It's Hard to Explain How Much We Have Lost

Talk to anyone with chronic pain, and they will tell you that the experience of unrelenting and debilitating pain feels impossible to explain. They will tell you that you can't understand it until it has happened to you. Similar to other life struggles, you don't get it until you get it. I have spent many hours trying to understand what makes chronic pain so difficult to understand, and I think one small piece of the puzzle is that it is hard to explain how much we have lost.

A friend and I were talking about life, and she shared how God took away the one thing she most wanted. She wanted this thing, and God said no. She asked me if I felt the same way about my chronic pain. "I know you used to love the outdoors, and now you can't be outside in the ways you want to," she said. "Do you also feel like God took away the thing you most wanted?"

I said yes. But then I said no, because that is not the best way to describe it. Not being able to work and play outside is a difficult loss, but I can't say that chronic pain took the one thing that I loved and most wanted. It seems more accurate to say that at different times it has taken almost everything away. Chronic pain doesn't take one or two or three things away. Many times, we lose our first dream, our second dream, our third dream, and most of the ones that follow.

The losses of chronic pain are not worse than other life losses. They are merely different. I believe the main difference is that when we lose the ability to move our bodies, we lose our freedom and our power to choose. We are constricted and confined, imprisoned and controlled by the whims of our physical bodies. We lose our freedom to physically carry out our plans and dreams. We lose our freedom to walk out the door, go on vacation, and do our chores. We lose our freedom to move, sit, walk, and go to the places we want to go.

Life and everything it contains, every corner, crevice, piece and part of who we are and how we relate to the surrounding world, become tainted when our bodies fail to work as they should. During those seasons when my pain was most severe, I felt as though I lived in a vacuum of nothingness. Me and the couch, the couch and me, and occasional trips to the bathroom and kitchen. This felt like the extent of my world. And for many people with chronic pain, this state is not a passing season, but a constant way of living for decades into a lifetime.

We grew up dreaming of a life of movement and laughter, family and friends, children and play, career and adventure. We grew up imagining we would contribute and help and socialize and enjoy the good things God provides. And then one day, we find ourselves alone on the couch in agony. We find ourselves staring at the TV, whiling away the hours until we can hopefully sleep through the pain, just so we can wake up to another day exactly the same as the one before. It is hard to explain how much we have lost.

Physical Loss is Just the Beginning

Approximately 100 million adults in the United States experience chronic pain that is moderate or severe, or that limits them in a way that affects their ability to work.[1] For these individuals, the life we once lived, the one in which we could choose to get up and move whenever and however we desire, is gone. Spontaneity and freedom of movement are things of the past. Depending on the nature of our condition, perhaps lying still is difficult, or perhaps it is sitting that causes us unbearable pain. Whatever physical tasks it may be – bending, walking, lifting, kneeling, eating, typing, and so on – we used to be able to do them and now we cannot.

And from the physical loss flows all other manner of loss. Difficulty with movement affects *every* single area of life. Daily tasks

6

of living such as doing laundry and preparing dinner now range from inconvenient to impossible. Activities that never seemed "physical" in the past wear us thin and suck us dry.

In the italicized paragraphs throughout the rest of this chapter, you will find true stories of individuals with chronic illness and pain, describing what they have lost.

Every few weeks I spend a morning braiding my daughter's hair into cornrows. The day after, I crash. I am unable to do anything but lie in bed for the next two days, because the exertion of holding my arms up for so long takes away all my strength.

During my second pregnancy I felt I had lost nearly everything. The pain started before I even knew I was pregnant, and it got bad fast. It was extremely debilitating. I had to sit in a reclined position with my feet up at all times and walk with a cane. I listened to audio books all day, every day. I can't express in words how difficult that was.

Pain makes even the simple act of walking difficult for me. That makes it hard to clean, cook, and shop. For example, shopping for clothing becomes a task to get done as quickly as possible. Chronic pain does not allow for pleasure shopping, or even checking different places for price comparisons. With chronic pain, I go to one store. I buy the first thing that even remotely works, and that has to be good enough.

Work, Service, and Leisure Loss

Our physical losses and limitations lead to work, career, service, and recreational losses. Some of us retain the ability to maintain previous commitments, while others become housebound or even bedbound. For almost all, the ability to work, serve, and play is greatly diminished. A survey of individuals with chronic pain in Europe found that 19% experienced job loss, 13% were forced to find new jobs that better accommodated their pain, and 61% felt that their work outside of the home had been affected in some way.[2]

We realize that we used to have it "all," because now we are forced to choose. We have to choose between going to work or caring for our children, attending girl's night or cleaning the house, making dinner for our family or going to church. Every day we face the difficult task of deciding which of our commitments are most important, letting go of things that are good, but not quite necessary.

The most painful has been the loss of my career. With it, I lost my sense of identity and purpose. I had enjoyed success in my work and had great pride in my accomplishments. I was mainly raised by a single mother who stressed the importance of self-reliance and independence. If I couldn't work and support myself, then what value did I have? That is how I saw it, and it has been a long road to accepting that loss and reshaping my ideas of self-worth.

I studied for years with plans to be a psychologist. Partway into my dissertation, I was hospitalized due to my symptoms and had to quit. I lost all momentum, and once I stabilized, the only work I could find was as a secretary. After several months at this job I was fired for taking too many sick days. Now I am unemployed, and I don't know what to do.

Relationship and Community Loss

Our friendships are hit hard. We live in a world that does not stop, and when we can no longer keep up, we get left behind. A few stay, but most do not want to engage in the slower, less exciting life we now live. Friendships that were grounded in shared activities quickly fade when we can't participate in the hiking or dancing or parties that drew our friend groups together in the first place. Other friendships are lost because some people are frightened by our suffering, unsure how to respond to our suffering, or forget about our suffering.

Not only do we lose friends, but we struggle to foster a sense of community at all because we have trouble going to the places where community happens. Getting to church becomes difficult to impossible. Attending important events or get-togethers becomes a burdensome task that requires days to weeks of advance planning. The more we struggle to leave the house, the more relationships go uncultivated and the more we find ourselves spending our days alone.

Every single one of my friends left me when I became sick. Every. single. one. At first they were supportive and helped me, but they were unable to understand why I never got better. They told me I

8

was bringing these health problems on myself and to give them a call when I stopped faking.

Marriage and Family Loss

Family dynamics change when pain and illness come to stay. Our marriages change. There is nothing romantic about severe chronic pain, and its effects pervade even the strongest relationship. Depending on the severity of our pain, spouses may transition from partner to caretaker, soon buckling under the strain of managing the work we can no longer complete.

Our ability to become parents and function as parents is affected. Some individuals with chronic pain are unable to conceive or care for a child. For those who do have families, parenting becomes much more difficult.

Some of my toughest losses come from witnessing how my illnesses and pain affect my family. For example, I have to stop my little girl from running into me at full speed for a hug. My heart breaks when she says things like "I wish I had a magic wand to take away all your pain."

It saddens me that I can't be the adventurous and active woman my husband married. We had so many dreams that centered around travel and seeing the world. Many of those activities are now very difficult and sometimes impossible. This is so painful to accept and process as a young adult.

My husband left me several years after I was diagnosed. He told me I was holding him back.

The divorce rates of couples in which one spouse has a long-term health condition are notoriously high, and multiple studies conclude that women have a much higher risk of being abandoned. One study of patients diagnosed with a brain tumor or multiple sclerosis found that woman are six times more likely to be abandoned by a spouse after diagnosis than men.[3]

Financial Loss

Chronic pain is expensive. Chronic pain is also so devastating that we are willing to pay just about anything to get rid of it. The bills pile up, with the total national cost of health care for chronic pain in the United States totaling more than the cost of treating heart disease, cancer, and diabetes combined.[1] Payment after payment is shelled out, often with little relief.

And as the bills pile up, chronic pain diminishes our ability to work for an income to pay them. Depending on our level of disability, we may be forced to quit working, find a less stressful and less paying line of work, or greatly decrease our hours. Spouses and family members may be forced to quit their jobs to care for us. This deadly combination of increased bills and decreased income can lead to financial ruin.

The monthly cost for my health care, all of which is medically necessary for me to live, is over $20,000 a month. Who can afford that? I have health insurance, but they don't want to pay for the treatments I need.

Loss of Self

Perhaps the most damaging loss of chronic pain is the way it takes away our sense of self and erases the person we once thought ourselves to be. When our bodies fail to work as they should, we transition from confident and capable to uncertain and filled with self-doubt. We are overly aware that we are inept in areas where we used to excel, and this fills us with feelings of inadequacy and shame.

Mentally, pain reduces our ability to think, concentrate, and make decisions. Emotionally, many of us are not the same person. As our mental health regresses because we are living in a state of constant physical stress, doctors begin to blame our physical pain on our emotional instability, failing to realize many of us were emotionally healthy until chronic pain came along and took everything away.

I read somewhere that those with chronic pain and illness have to grieve the loss of two separate lives. I've had to grieve the loss of the person I once was and also grieve the future self that I assumed I'd have.

10

When pain and suffering came and never left, I lost my faith. I don't know who I am without the faith of my childhood.

Sometimes, I think I have almost lost my sanity.

A Being Who Is Loss

Chronic pain and illness strip us naked and bare until the person we once were exists as a distant shadow, a bright and joyful figure from the past, forever gone as we once were. So many losses accumulate into one huge loss that says we can't have any of the things we want in life. Just one of these losses would be burden enough. The devastation of losing a job, career, or livelihood. The heartbreak of never again running, jumping, dancing, or living out a passion. The loss of financial security, relationships, marriages, and our sense of who we are. Any of these losses alone would be devastating, and often unnoticed is the fact that we have experienced loss in every part of our world.

Each day seems to hold new manifestations of this pain's presence in our lives that stop us from doing what we want and being who we want. It doesn't seem right and it doesn't seem fair. Knowing how to respond to the emotional pain of so many losses – each one crushing down on top of the other, defying our ability to breath – feels impossible. What do we do when everything has been taken away?

Chapter 1 Journaling Question

1. What has chronic pain or illness taken from you? Before reading the next chapter, write out a detailed list of everything you have lost.

CHAPTER 2

Encountering God in Our Grief

What was it like thinking through all that you have lost because of chronic illness and pain? When I read my own list, it hurts my heart and I feel an ache in my gut. My list of losses fills me with painful memories, deep emotions, and confusing questions.

The memories are first to arise. I remember the counseling job I had to leave, the swing of the door behind me as I wondered if my body would ever be able to work more than a few hours a week again. I think of the long walks I used to take with my husband through the woods, the talking and laughing for miles and miles that is not quite possible to replicate in the stillness of a living room. There was the feeling that came when I used to run down the road, a sharp breeze on my face, ragged breath and burning muscles telling me I was alive. Sometimes I used to stand at the kitchen table for hours, fashioning pierogis from homemade dough, as I waited for the bread to finish baking. Once upon a time I used to get up whenever I desired to do whatever I desired.

As these memories flash through my mind, I am reminded, yet again, how much chronic pain has taken. The feeling of loss is always present, lingering in the background, but sometimes it hits me harder than normal. Sometimes it comes with a sudden jolt, and a cloud of emotions overwhelms me. I feel angry, frustrated, and confused. I feel a flash of guilt and a flicker of envy. Sometimes, for just a moment, I smile at the memories of moving and running and doing, but then I am overwhelmed by a crushing feeling of sadness.

Then, the questions. So many questions. *Why me? What is the purpose of all of this loss? How could this possibly turn out for my good? God, how could you do this to me? Why didn't you stop it? God, are you listening to me? This just isn't fair!*

I close my eyes and envision these memories, emotions, and questions as a whirling and intangible force that builds up inside of my heart. This force is so overwhelming that I start to wonder, *where do I put it? Where do I put this whirlwind of loss that takes up so much space?* These emotions that stay locked up inside. These unanswered questions that overtake my thoughts. These painful memories that are triggered every time I see someone run down the road. *If I don't find somewhere to put them, perhaps I will explode!*

Do you feel these same losses building up inside, just as I do? Can you feel the way they press outward, ever-growing, ever-intensifying in new ways each day? Somehow, these emotions, questions, and memories must be released from the stronghold of our hearts, or all of us may burst.

I believe this release happens through the process of grieving and mourning all that has been taken away. Grieving happens when we recognize and take hold of all that we feel, question, and remember. We take all of this loss in our hands – refusing to keep it inside in an act of stoicism, resisting the urge to hurl it at the nearest and safest human target – and instead, we honestly and transparently speak it before a God who hears us and responds to us in our pain. Grief is the process by which we actively release all that we feel, question, and remember at the feet of God and the people he has placed in our lives.

The Ugliness of Grief

Standing before God in the raw and unfiltered state of grief is terrifying. So much vulnerability is required to expose these parts of ourselves that we would rather keep hidden away. The emotions I feel in the midst of chronic pain are not pretty. They are ugly and, at times, expressed in sinful ways. The questions I have about my pain are not nice. They are angry and filled with doubt. My memories of chronic pain are not processed or understood. They are desperate and confusing and not-yet-redeemed. To be honest about *all* that I feel, question, and remember can feel wrong, perhaps even sinful. Who am I to speak to God in this way?

I think of a passionate and courageous woman I once counseled. She sits across from me and bares her soul about the painful loss she has experienced in one of her relationships. Her face is red and her eyes are filled with tears as she tells me she is filled with an anger that might overcome her. Sadness, shame, guilt, and fear overwhelm her. "I just need to stop feeling this way," she says. "These emotions are too much for me to handle. Everyone is telling me I can't let my emotions take over. I need to think about this logically."

She wants logic. Is this the answer? She wants perfect control of her emotions. Is this really the remedy? When a baby dies or a wife is unfaithful or a job is lost or chronic pain crashes down like a wall stopping us in our tracks. Is the answer to all of this less emotions and more logic?

This woman was not the first to sit across from me and tell me she is scared of her emotions and all that she feels. She was not the first churched woman to tell me that perhaps she shouldn't be feeling everything so strongly. In the face of devastating loss, our emotions can become so strong that it feels like something is wrong with us. Feelings like this can't possibly be okay or godly, and we fear if we let them persist, the intensity might overtake us.

The Proper and Normal Responses to Pain

But there is a reason we feel the way we feel. The reality of here and now is that evil and suffering are rampant in our world and our lives, and the *proper* response to these things is sorrow and mourning. We have not yet arrived. We are not yet at the final destination where the old order of things will pass away and we will never weep or wail again. And until we are there, we *must* wail and we *must* weep when things of this world overcome us.

Mourning and sorrow are the proper responses when bad things happen. How do we so easily forget this simple truth? When Jesus saw Lazarus dead in the tomb, he wept even though he knew Lazarus would soon be alive and all would be redeemed in the end. He wept in the face of death and suffering and pain, just as he would later celebrate when all was restored. Why? Because weeping, sorrow, and grief are the proper responses to suffering, pain, and loss.

But, let's take this a step further. Even when our feelings and responses to pain are not "proper," so to speak, they are often normal, expected, and understandable. The *normal* responses to pain and loss that we all feel are anger and confusion, doubt and fear, guilt and shame. If we don't allow ourselves to feel whatever we feel, whether good or bad, holy or sinful, true or false, we will never work through our emotions to learn how they can become glorifying to God. We process these normal responses, not by shutting them down, but by speaking them aloud, allowing God and those around us to guide us back to truth.

Only through speaking what is actually on our minds and not what we think should be on our minds can God guide us to where he wants us to be. So often we know where we should be, but we aren't there yet. We don't feel what we think we should feel. We are still asking questions when we want to be able to trust. We are still doubting that past memories of pain have any purpose or will ever be redeemed. And God, in his grace, meets us here. Right here. Not where we should be or want to be, but where we are. Are we willing to meet with him?

Encountering God through Questions and Doubt

Are you willing to meet with God in your loss and grief? We all respond differently to our suffering. For some, our pain draws us closer to God. For others, this pain makes him feel distant and uncaring.

I have never run away from God or abandoned my faith because of my pain. This has not been my story. I do not believe this is because of any great faith I hold. I believe it is because I see no other option than God. If I left, where would I go? I am unable to *not* believe that God exists, and if the God of the Bible exists then how can I run? Where would I run to? The world has nothing for me. God has marked me as his own, and I could not leave if I wanted.

My story is not one of running, but of fear, anger, and brokenness, even as I stay. I believe it is accurate to say that large portions of my relationship with God over the past five years have been forged on the fragile framework of questions, confusion, and doubt. But as I look back, I wonder if this framework is not quite as fragile as I once thought.

I believe that all of our confusion and doubt in the face of loss and pain can serve as a fierce reminder of our need for a God who has the answers to the questions that haunt us, even if we will never be privy to his thoughts and ways. I believe our questions can be the reason we turn to God with a renewed fervor to understand this faith we so long took for granted when life was going as planned. How could we not want to be closer to the One who knows all that we do not know?

I wonder what would happen if, like Job, we refused to be silent in our suffering. In the midst of incalculable loss, Job, a great man of

16

God, calls out, "Therefore I will not keep silent; I will speak out in the anguish of my spirit, I will complain in the bitterness of my soul" (Job 7:11). This, I believe, is the essence of our grief. Refusing to be silent. Speaking aloud our anguish. Openly declaring the bitterness in our souls that we are afraid to admit is there. We simply talk to God, when we would rather walk away.

Job lost everything, his wealth and his family, his health and his friends. And in his suffering, Job did not mince words, water down the extent of his experience, or hold back his forceful thoughts. Instead, he spoke the uncensored truth of his suffering, knowing he had questions that only his Creator could answer. I wonder what would happen if you spoke your questions to God, like Job did.

"Why have you made me your target?
Have I become a burden to you?
…Does it please you to oppress me,
to spurn the work of your hands,
while you smile on the plans of the wicked?
…Your hands shaped me and made me
Will you now turn and destroy me?"
(Job 7:20b, 10:3, 10:8).

Have you ever approached God to ask him why he allowed this loss into your life? Have you ever allowed yourself to ask, "Why me?"

I suppose "Why not me?" might be the more theologically correct question, but don't you still want to know? Don't you want to get that question off your chest? Don't you want to speak these words before the God who allowed pain and illness into your life? I do.

It doesn't matter how much I read and know about the theology of suffering. As much as I know I deserve to be placed in the depths of hell for my sin, as much as I know that there is nothing in me that is worthy of good health, as much as I know that God is sovereign, good, all-knowing and always makes the right decisions, I still want to ask. I wonder what in the world God was thinking when he allowed this pain into my life. And so I ask.

God, why me?
God, are you sure this isn't a mistake?
God, have you forgotten me?
God, are you still there?

God, can you explain what in the world is going on?

I ask because God allows me to ask. I ask because it is these desperate and unanswerable questions that draw me towards God with an insatiable need to know and understand his unfathomable ways. It is my own inability to understand and know his ways that draws me to the One who holds the heavens and the earth, my life and yours, in the palm of his hands. Sometimes angry and sometimes timid, I come before God and ask. I ask because I can. I can because he loves me. He loves me enough to let me ask.

He allows our questions, but if we are to question God, we must be ready for his response. When God responds to Job, he appeals to his own nature and character, reminding us of who he is and who we are questioning.

> "Brace yourself like a man;
> I will question you,
> and you shall answer me.
> Would you discredit my justice?
> Would you condemn me to justify yourself?
> Do you have an arm like God's,
> and can your voice thunder like his?"
> (Job 38:3; 40:8,9).

When we request a meeting with God, asking him questions that may not have answers that are of this earth, he often gives us something better than answers. He gives us a reminder of who he is and who we are questioning. He reminds us of his all-powerful and holy character, and of our weakness before him. And to this reminder Job responds with a new and humbled understanding.

> "Surely I spoke of things I did not understand,
> things too wonderful for me to know"
> (Job, 42:3b).

Job never discovered the reason for his suffering, yet in the midst of not knowing, he received a better gift, that of encountering God. Job was reminded of the gift of simply being in God's presence, a presence he never would have entered if he had never asked his questions that ended up having no answers. Yet as he approached

God, his anger and bitterness were softened by simply being in the presence of the Almighty One who knows all things.

In our asking we draw near to God with a deep need to know what might not be knowable. It is in our not knowing that God invites us to come, to trust, to depend. In our asking, we draw near to him, even when he chooses to withhold the information that seemed so pertinent at first, but now feels secondary to simply being in relationship with the One who knows.

Longing to Run

Let me share with you how this process of encountering God has played out in my own life. I used to feel angry every time I saw someone run down the road because it reminded me of all the ways I used to be active. I would be driving through our community and, inevitability, a stranger would jog or sprint by. My heart would pound within my chest and then leap into my throat. Sometimes I would cry. My mind would flash back to when I used to be healthy, energetic, and physically resilient. Underneath my anger dwelled sadness, jealousy, and dissatisfaction with my life.

For a long time, my strategy for getting through these moments was to distract myself. I would push the feelings away and pretend they were not there. I would turn my gaze and think about something else, but this strategy never worked for long. I wanted to feel content with the life I had been given. I wanted to feel happy instead of jealous when other people did what they loved. I knew exactly where I needed to be, but I didn't know how to get there.

Everything changed the day I asked myself who I was angry with. I realized I wasn't angry with the innocent stranger on a jog. I wasn't angry with myself or any other person. I was angry with God and the way he had orchestrated my life. My jealousy had nothing to do with the person running down the road. It was the fruit of my dissatisfaction with what God had given and not given me.

From that day forward I changed my strategy. Instead of distracting myself and trying to think about something else, I began to engage with all that I was feeling. I felt the anger and the sadness. I allowed memories of when I used to be active flood my mind. And I spoke to God about what I was feeling and experiencing.

God, I hate this. It hurts and it isn't fair. I used to be able to do so much, and now I cannot. I know you could fix this in an instant, but

19

you haven't, and that makes me angry. I am sad and frustrated and confused. Why is this what you want for my life? What purpose could you possibly have? Running and moving are good things. They are not evil or harmful to others. I don't know how to deal with this. I don't know what to do. I don't want to feel like this all the time, but this is where I am.

As I purposefully approached God, he began to change my heart. It is hard to describe or know exactly what happened. I just know that as I spoke to God and engaged my grief instead of pushing it away, I slowly began to accept the limitations he had placed in my life. As I prayed, he began to give me a desire to trust him. He led me to Scripture that spoke to my heart and gave me peace and hope. He began to bring me where I knew I needed to be from the beginning, but hadn't known how to get there on my own.

I still cry about my inability to run and be active, but it no longer overcomes me. I no longer feel angry or jealous. I just feel sad because exercise and physical activity are good things I lost, and I will probably remain sad about them until the day I die. And this is okay. This is where I am in my ongoing process of grief, and God meets me and stays with me here.

Chapter 2 Journaling Questions

1. The nature of grief is that it is unfiltered. It is an expression of our uncensored emotions, questions, and memories. If we try to filter our grief by taking away the parts that are messy or the parts that we think shouldn't be there, then it isn't grief anymore; rather, it has turned into our logical take of the situation.

    As you come before God with your questions, emotions, and memories, are you filtering or censoring yourself? If so, what do you believe prevents you from being completely honest with God?

2. What questions do you have for God? In any other relationship, questions of doubt and uncertainty would place a wedge between the questioner and the one being questioned. But not with God. He is too gracious, loving, and forgiving, and he invites us to ask. What questions do you have for the holy and all-knowing God?

3. What three emotions are you most aware of as you think of everything that chronic pain or illness has taken away? Describe what is it like to experience these emotions.

4. What memories most haunt you? Write out the events in your past that bring you to tears and doubt and confusion.

CHAPTER 3

Rituals of Grief

Grief is the process by which we actively release all that we feel, question, and remember at the feet of God and the people he has placed in our lives. This is how I defined grief in the last chapter. But, I also recognize this definition doesn't do justice to the subjective and expansive nature of grief, which manifests in different ways for different people. Everybody grieves differently. One way to think about grief is to see it as an active ritual. Our rituals of grief vary, but they serve the same purpose.

Several years ago I had one of my major flares. When my pain flares to higher than average intensity, I struggle to keep up with my schedule. Life feels overwhelming, and every night I wonder if I will be able to make it through my responsibilities the next day. During this particular flare, I was simultaneously experiencing other significant stressors, and life felt more than I could handle.

Throughout this season, I found myself taking time every day to put on praise and worship music, lie down on the living room floor, and cry as I listened. Doing this was extremely uncharacteristic of me. I don't listen to music of any kind unless I am driving or someone else happens to be playing music in the background. The act of taking a specific time each day to do so was a strange shift from my normal habits and way of doing things.

At the time, it felt random, but looking back, it makes perfect sense. Each day I was engaging in intentional grieving, even though I did not realize what I was doing at the time. Each day, I was releasing all that I felt through my tears. Each day, I was lying down to listen to words of truth spoken through music that would not normally be a part of my day. Adding this ritual to my daily life was the active means I was using to lay all of my loss before God when life was too much to handle.

Crying while listening to praise and worship music is one way I have grieved through one difficult season of my life. It provides a picture of what grief often looks like – messy, intentional, active, and practiced regularly. This example also demonstrates how sometimes we are engaged in practices of grief without realizing we are doing so.

How about you? How do you grieve? Think back over the last months and years of pain and illness and consider if you have already knowingly or unknowingly added rituals of grief to your life. It's okay if you can't think of any. Throughout this chapter I will provide examples of what grieving sometimes looks like, and from these examples you can come up with your own rituals and practices.

Speaking Our Chronic Pain Stories Aloud

Just as we lay our grief at the feet of God, we can also lay our grief at the feet of the people in our lives through speaking our stories of pain aloud.

When I counsel individuals who are grieving, we often spend several sessions talking about what has been lost and how this has affected them. I help those sitting in front of me remember the good memories and the bad, the past and present feelings, what happened and how they responded. In these moments of listening to their story, I sometimes feel a transfer of energy, as though through the act of telling their story, they are handing some of their grief over to me. They leave feeling a little lighter, and I am left to carry the tiniest portion of their load.

Sharing the details of your pain or illness with another person can be difficult and frightening. We wonder, "Will they judge me? Will they believe my pain is real? How will they respond?" But in the end I believe it is worth it. Here is how one of my friends put it.

I have found that sharing my losses with a close and understanding friend can help immensely. I spent years hiding the severity and frequency of my pain from my family, friends, and coworkers. I was basically living a double life and had two extreme ways of existing. Full-speed or laid out.

It was exhausting and isolating because I felt like nobody truly knew or understood me. How could they? I was hiding it and doing all those things we are urged to do our entire lives. "Push through, pick yourself up, forge ahead." Until I couldn't. I did those things until my body completely revolted and pretending was no longer an option.

So now I find that it helps me to just speak the truth to somebody about what I'm going through. It has been a long process for me to feel comfortable discussing my pain, even with those closest to me. People can be judgmental and say hurtful things when faced with something they can't see or fully understand. I've been on the receiving end of many hurtful words. My response was to give up, shut down, and bury the reality of my pain.

Finally, I began opening up and speaking to God about my struggles. Prayer became a comforting ritual. Then I got very real with my husband about how much I was suffering. That was the point when I expressed my inability to continue working. Finally, I slowly started talking to my friends and even made new ones online. I now have a handful of people that I can trust with this very vulnerable piece of me.

Telling our story to people we trust is a crucial part of grieving our losses. There are so many ways to do this. Here are some ideas to get you started.

Schedule a specific and purposeful time to
tell your story to a friend_____

See a counselor_____

If you aren't ready to talk to someone,
write your losses and sorrows in a journal_____

Share your story in a public setting_____

Find others going through the same situation
and share your stories back and forth_____

Start a blog, write a book, or share your story
through some form of art_____

Pray your story aloud, telling God every single
detail of what you have been through from
beginning to end _____

Grieving Through Creative Expression

At times, it can feel impossible to process all that we are feeling
and experiencing through speaking mere words. Sometimes more is
needed. Sometimes chronic pain defies description, and our internal
turmoil transcends everyday language. Our emotions become a
convoluted mess that we do not even understand for our own selves,
let alone feel capable of describing to someone else. In these cases,
one of the best ways to express ourselves is through creating and
consuming various forms of art.

Writing is my form of creative expression. Writing is the way I
sort through my tangled thoughts and emotions, often writing things I
didn't know I think or feel until the words leave my fingertips and
appear on the computer screen. In 2014 I started a blog, and I never
could have imagined the healing that would occur through carefully
forming posts for other people going through similar situations to
read. Every time I wrote, I felt a small release of grief. Every time
someone responded saying they felt the same way, I felt a comradery
that brought healing to my soul. Every time I was able to describe
something in writing that felt impossible to accurately explain when
speaking aloud, I felt validated and confirmed. Writing within
community is one of the ways I continuously grieve my losses.

For some people, music becomes extremely important. One
individual with chronic pain remarks, "One way I grieve is through
singing songs. There are a few in particular that have gotten me
through hard times, but 'God Moves in Mysterious Ways' definitely
stands out. I have sung that at least a thousand times."

Any form of creative expression can be used to process
underlying emotions, thoughts, and beliefs that we do not fully
understand. Painting, drawing, sculpting, music, coloring, crafts,
sewing, knitting, embroidery, ceramics, graphic design, acting…the
options are endless. In the same way, sometimes art that other people
have created speaks to our experience when we are unable to find our
own words. Do not underestimate the healing powers of creative
expression, even if you do not consider yourself a particularly creative
person.

Find or write a song that gives words to
your experience_____

Write a poem, essay, play, book, or comic script
that describes your life with chronic
illness and pain_____

Create a painting, drawing, sculpture, craft,
collage or any other work of art that describes
what you feel physically and/or emotionally
in the midst of your illness and pain_____

Visit the website PainExhibit.org and find
the work of art that best describes your experience_____

Processing Chronic Pain and Illness Memories

Sometimes, processing our experiences in the moment can feel impossible. In the day to day of illness and pain, our focus is on survival. We only have enough space in our minds to think about the here and the now and how we will get through to the end of the day.

Not until we have a moment to breathe are we able to look back and fully comprehend what we have been through. Often, it is not until I have a season of lower pain levels or a season of higher internal strength that I am able to truly ponder the reality of my suffering and how it has affected me.

Chronic pain and illness can bring about memories that are truly traumatic. Perhaps you have had a near death experience or a surgery that went horribly wrong. Perhaps you experienced a hospital stay with inadequate treatment or care, leading to terrible health consequences. Some individuals with chronic pain and illness are abandoned, labeled as addicts, or thrown out of their homes with accusations of malingering.

Maybe you have had seasons when your pain was so devastating and oppressive that you attempted to take your own life. Perhaps you have been denied or can't afford treatment, leaving you sitting at home with severely unmanaged pain, unsure how to go on. We can only push memories such as these aside for so long before they surface, begging us to sit with them, process them, and respond to them.

Write a letter to your former self –
who you were before chronic pain and illness
became a part of your life_____

What memories are you unable to get out of your head?
Tell someone about them or write out what
you remember_____

Write a letter to the doctor, nurse, surgeon,
friend, family member, or stranger who hurt you
or who holds responsibility for worsening your
pain or illness_____

Look at pictures and reminders of who you
used to be. Let yourself cry at the loss and
smile at what you used to be able to do_____

Write out a balanced list of both good and
bad memories from your last year of pain and
illness. It is healthy to purposefully remember
both the good and the bad_____

Journal an answer to this question: How has
God redeemed the suffering and tragedy
you have experienced?_____

Making the Laments of Scripture Our Own

The grief hits me hardest right after I experience a relapse. Every time I relapse after making significant progress, I experience a devastating blow that never gets easier to handle. Every single time, I have to deal with the knowledge that it will take me months to climb out again. All the losses I have grieved in the past rise up again to haunt me. I have to do the hard work of mourning them over and over again.

One of these relapses happened in October of 2014 when I got stuck in traffic and then lost in a downpour on the way home from a doctor's appointment that lasted much longer than originally expected. Sitting and standing for too long that day was enough to trigger a relapse that would take the next year to pull through back to regular pain levels. The weeks following this setback were dark and devastating. They were filled with sobbing and pain, as I thought about all the hard work I had done to bring healing to my body, only for hopes of continued progress to be taken away in a moment.

I remember turning to Lamentations 3. I read this chapter over and over again, finding words that described where I was in the moment. I needed words that described darkness and pain. I needed words that helped the tears come to my eyes. I needed just a little bit of hope, but not too much, or else I wouldn't be able to believe it was true. And I found all of this in Lamentations 3. I made this lament my own by writing the whole chapter in my journal and forming my own response to each verse.

What passage in Scripture speaks to you? What lament in Scripture gives words to your pain and experience? Read through the Psalms, Job, the Gospels, and the Old Testament prophets. Find the passage that makes you think "That is exactly how I feel!" Find the passage that describes your story and where you are in this season of life.

Read it over and over again. Write it out in a journal. Add your own thoughts and feelings and understanding of the passage. Speak it aloud to God, and let it direct your prayers towards him. Know that you are not alone in your lament. Let the words of life found in God's Holy Book bring healing to your soul. As you read through Scripture, pick one passage to be your own. If you are struggling to know where to start, consider looking at these Psalms: Psalm 38, Psalm 77, Psalm 88, Psalm 142. Choose one or more of the following ways to interact with your passage.

Memorize your passage of Scripture_____

Rewrite your Scripture in your own words_____

Pray your passage of Scripture aloud_____

Copy your passage of Scripture into a journal_____

Use your passage of Scripture as the basis for creating a work of art_____

31

Journal your thoughts, feelings,
and understanding of the passage_____

Creating Our Own Personal Grieving Rituals

In the end, I think we all come up with grieving rituals that make sense to us. Over time this becomes an intuitive process – whatever comes to mind is the right thing to do, even if it feels silly or strange. Here are some additional ideas.

Write a letter to your chronic illness or pain.
If you could say anything to your pain,
what would it be?_____

Spend time alone in nature_____

Acknowledge anniversaries and milestones
each year – both the good and the bad – by
lighting a candle, going to a particular place,
buying a bottle of wine, watching a specific
movie, or any number of activities_____

Create a list, drawing, journal entry, or collage
of the person you want to be in the midst of
your pain and illness _____

Write out a reverse bucket list of all the things
you have been able to do in life before the
pain and in spite of the pain_____

A Lifelong Practice

I believe that grief should be a lifelong practice that we intentionally incorporate into our daily lives of illness and pain. Our diseases and conditions may shift and change in intensity across seasons, but they are always constantly present. We mourn our losses because there is no way to fix our losses or get our old lives back. There is no way *not* to experience the pain, and so in grief, we dive in headfirst, experiencing our pain to the fullest extent, that we might know it, understand it, and move through it, believing God is with us every step of the way.

Chapter 3 – Journaling Questions

1. What rituals of grief, if any, have you already incorporated into your life? If you can't think of any, that's okay!

2. Go back through the examples given in this chapter and choose one or two rituals of grief you would like to add to your life. Write them below and come up with a plan for where and when you will carry them out.

CHAPTER 4

The Man Who Has God for His Treasure

I sometimes play a game in my mind. Perhaps a good name for it would be *If I Hadn't...* I think of all the small building blocks that led up to my pain and prevented my pain from being healed. I think of all the things I wish I had done, the things I wish I knew. So many small decisions led me to where I am today. On so many occasions, if *I just hadn't,* I imagine I wouldn't still be in pain.

First, a small injury weakened my body. *If I hadn't* gone to that hot yoga class and stretched too far... *If I hadn't* done that yoga pose incorrectly for weeks without realizing my posture was wrong... *If I hadn't* done these things, I wouldn't have weakened the ligaments in my low back, setting the stage for disaster.

Disaster came in the form of a chiropractor. Just out of school, working her first job, she made a mistake that would be the beginning of my descent into constant pain. She shoved down hard on the left side, just below the small of my back, as I lay on a drop table that was synched too tight. A sudden sharp pain. My gut told me something was terribly wrong, but she told me it was fine. So, I kept seeing her over and over again, not realizing she was tearing the ligaments that connect my sacrum and ilium on both sides of my pelvis.

Sacroiliac joint dysfunction. It sounds like such an innocuous name for a condition that brought my life to a screeching halt. After her adjustments, my sacroiliac joints, which are supposed to be held tightly in place by ligaments with just a little bit of give, would never be the same. The ligaments now hang loose, leading to misalignment, inflammation, and pain.

And I wonder. *If I hadn't* moved to Baltimore and left the chiropractor I trusted behind... *If I hadn't* gone on that particular day when she adjusted a man three times bigger than me and then forgot to loosen the drop table to a setting appropriate to my weight... *If I hadn't* ignored my gut that was screaming at me to stop seeing her...

It took me years following this injury to fully understand the reality of my new physical limitations. It seemed inconceivable that I couldn't walk too far or sit too long without re-injuring myself. I followed the advice so often given to "just push through," and it led to sharp regression. Over and over again, as I tried to live normal life, I put more wear and tear on my ligaments, leading to more damage. More tearing, more stretching, more spraining. Each re-injury pushed me further and further down until I learned how to effectively pace myself. But the irreparable damage was already done.

All of my major setbacks and relapses came from activities I wish I hadn't done. And I can't help but wonder. *If I hadn't* walked miles and miles touring Washington, DC that one day... *If I hadn't* been ignorant to the fact that the nature of my injury means I should *never, ever* have done all that vacuuming... *If I hadn't* helped with packing and carrying boxes when we moved... *If I hadn't* gone to that disastrous doctor's appointment that went too long and then gotten lost on the way home...

There are more *if I hadn'ts* than I can count. It is easy for me to blame myself and tell myself it is my fault for every "mistake" that pushed me further into pain. But the nature of this condition is that I never know if it was a "mistake" until it is too late. I don't know until it has happened.

The Things We Wouldn't Have

But if I could have made all the right decisions and stopped this downward spiral, would I have done so? So much would be at stake. I can only play this game for a few seconds in my mind before I realize...

If I hadn't moved to Baltimore, I wouldn't be right where I feel like God wants me to be. I wouldn't be at the job and the church and the community that I know are supposed to be a part of my life. *If I hadn't* gone to that chiropractor and pain had never entered my life, some of my best friends would be unknown to me. Without pain, I never would have felt compelled to write. I never would have learned the compassion needed to meet the people I counsel in their pain. I would probably be a lot more selfish and a lot less empathetic. I wouldn't know half the things I now know.

If I hadn't done all of those things that led to re-injury, and my pain had been a short and passing season of life, I would be a different person. And if I had to choose between no pain and what God has done in my life through my pain...dare I say I would choose the pain? In many ways, I can't imagine the person I would be without it.

I am not alone in recognizing what pain and suffering has given me. Many of us are aware of blessings and good things in our lives that never would have come to be without our illness and pain. I appreciate what my friend, Charlene, has to say about this topic.

I am certain that I would not value my role as a mother in the same way if it were not for chronic pain. It is amazing to go through the amount of pain I have with pregnancy, and to look into the eyes of my girls, and without a hint of doubt, know that it was worth it. I would do it all again in a heartbeat. I really, truly value that gift.

I am also certain that I am less self-righteous and slower to judge others due to my experiences with chronic pain. When you go through something like this for years, trust me, you have extremely ugly moments. You fight for your faith hard, and sometimes you're afraid you are going to lose it.

Sometimes you question God. Sometimes you wonder if living in sin is better. Is that bad? Yes. Would I have thought myself capable of that? No. But pain has a way of revealing your heart, your weaknesses, and your unbelief. You work through so many things on a mental, emotional, and spiritual level, and still come out the other side with faith in Christ.

Tested faith, more precious than gold or silver. Pain has shown me my spiritual need and my own ugliness more than anything else, and due to that, I cling to the gospel and am much more hesitant to jump on others in judgement.

I have to agree with Charlene. Many of my own thoughts mirror her thoughts. This is a tricky game to play. So many conflicting feelings, as I consider both the things I have lost and the things I have gained. It is good to consider how chronic pain has changed us for the better. It is good to consider the blessings chronic pain has brought into our lives. But I can only be completely honest. For me, I am not sure these things I have gained are enough.

On their own, they *aren't* enough. Between the small glimpses of redemption are hours, days, and weeks of suffering that feel purposeless. My chronic pain hinders my ability to be the wife, sister, daughter, and friend that I want to be. Chronic pain severely limits my ability to work and serve. At times, chronic pain brings out the worst in me. The memories of my worst pain flares are seared into my mind, and they will never be erased. Severe, unending physical pain has wounded me, broken me, and I will never be the same.

And I have found that only God and the work of his Son, Jesus Christ, can truly bring hope to all the loss I have sustained. I will never be the same, but because God is my strength, I know I will never stop moving forward. I have been irrevocably marked by suffering and pain, but because Christ is my salvation, I am going to a place where pain and suffering will be no more. I will never stop feeling the hurt and curse of chronic pain; I will never "get over" my losses, but because I believe in a God who is sufficient, I know I have been given everything I will ever need for this lifetime.

All Things in One

Only God is enough to cover this loss, to make up for all chronic pain has taken away. Not the people we have met, the character we have built, or the good we have done that never would have happened without the pain. These are good things, but on their own, they are not enough.

There is a quote about this topic I have been trying to fully understand for some time. It is a quote that struck me from the first time I read it, that penetrated deep into my heart, that is so true, but left me asking...now what? What do I do with this? How do I *feel* this and *live* this out? In the Christian classic, *The Pursuit of God,* A. W. Tozer writes about the sufficiency of God in a way that has inspired and challenged me.

The man who has God for his treasure has all things in One. Many ordinary treasures may be denied him, or if he is allowed to have them, the enjoyment of them will be so tempered that they will never be necessary to his happiness. Or if he must see them go, one after one, he will scarcely feel a sense of loss, for having the Source of all things he has in One all satisfaction, all pleasure, all delight. Whatever he may lose he has actually lost nothing, for he now has it all in One. And has it purely, legitimately, and forever.[4]

Those who experience chronic pain are denied many of the ordinary treasures of life, some of the seemingly *basics* of life so easily taken for granted. We are denied the ability to move, socialize, serve, work, and play. We are denied the ability to live relationships to the fullest and carry out the goals and aspirations that previously drove us. Yet God has provided himself when all earthly treasures fade, "for having the Source of all things [we have] in One all satisfaction, all pleasure, all delight."

Living Before a Sufficient God

I believe God says he is enough for us, even when all else has been taken away. I believe this. But most of the time, if I am being honest with myself, he doesn't feel like enough. I'd like to have God and my health, God and my ability to move, God and my dreams for life. I have so far to go when it comes to living in light of God's sufficiency, yet a part of me knows – in this truth we find our hope.

I want to learn what it means to live before a sufficient God, believing and experiencing that he is enough for me. In a practical sense, I believe this begins when we bring our losses before God as Job did, engaging in a process that is relationship with God. Through this relationship we are given what we need to mourn everything we have lost. Through this relationship we learn to accept God as our all when everything is taken away. We have lost so much to our illness and pain, yet in our brokenness and suffering, we are given the opportunity to gain more of God than we ever had before.

When our pain is severe, we *will* get left behind by the rest of the world. We have to tearfully say no to things we want to do with people we want to see. We have to give up dreams and goals and careers and intended futures. We are left behind as everyone else forges ahead.

But God grants us a promise. Those who live with us may walk right past us in life, but God walks right alongside us. Our family and friends may move on when we are unable to participate in life, but God slows down to our pace. He stays no matter what. Our mother or father, sister, friend, doctor or church may forsake us, but the Lord will receive us every single time (Psalm 27:10). He will never falter, fade, or leave us, for he does not change like the shifting shadows, but is the same today, tomorrow, and for eternity.

He has always been there, right alongside us, yet for some of us, it is our chronic pain that shows us our need for him. Chronic pain is the fiery furnace we have been placed in that causes us to cry out for God to pluck us from the flames or at least grant us some superhuman strength to bear the fire. The trouble with the absence of pain is we begin to think we have control over the everyday workings of our bodies, when only through God do "we live and move and have our being" (Acts 17:28). But now, in our pain, limitation, and inability, we cry out with a deep and unquenchable need for God.

And so in our pain we go to him. We cry out and he hears us. We tell him our deepest thoughts and our most terrifying fears. He is the one we begin to weep and mourn with. With the Lord we laugh and smile at his unfathomable and humorous ways. We go to his Word for wisdom, encouragement, comfort, and strength. We come before him when the pain flares and we are uncertain if we can take it any longer. When we are uncertain if we can go on.

And it is here, in the deepest depths of our pain, that God points us to his Son. On those days when there are no answers, when no redemption or good can be seen with a human eye, we purposefully call to mind Christ and his work on this cross. We remember what he did for us. In the greatest act of love and mercy ever shown to mankind, he gave us what we do not deserve. In his perfection he bore the pain and punishment of our sins that we might freely accept his gift of life. Why would he do this for us? It doesn't make sense.

Yet, at the same time, it is the only thing that can possibly make sense when life is filled with pain. We are here, crying out, asking, "Why God? How could you let this pain happen?" And he gives no answer. Instead he shows us Christ who suffered for you and for me. And deep down in my heart, I know that anyone who would suffer the agony of the cross to save his enemies from death and eternal pain can only be a very good God who I can only trust.

Christine's Story

Christine is one of the people I never would have met without chronic pain, and I can't imagine life without her in it. I remember the day she reached out and emailed me after finding my blog. A few emails and Facebook posts here and there turned to texting every so often which turned to regular video chats about life and all those problems chronic pain causes on a daily basis.

Christine experiences constant pain due to degenerative disc disease, Sjogren's syndrome, osteoarthritis, neuropathy, and fibromyalgia. Once an active dancer, gymnast, traveler, and accountant, life began to change around the age of 25 when she first experienced low back pain after a long car trip. Soon the pain spread throughout her body and new issues began. Each year the severity and frequency of her pain increased, and like so many of us, Christine's life would never be the same. Listen to her story of seeking God in her pain in her own words:

"Before pain set in, I had idolized my self-sufficiency. My relationship with Jesus lacked any real depth. In my mind, God was around, but I didn't really need him because I was ultimately in control. I was certain that I could overcome any obstacle just by the sheer force of my own will and hard work. Well, chronic pain and illness don't always work that way. With each failed treatment protocol, I had to face the bitter fact that my pain wasn't something I could just decide to overcome. It wasn't like any career goals I had set where all I needed was a clear plan (usually in spreadsheet form) and some dedication.

As my body was breaking down, God was chipping away layers of my ego. I questioned God and his purpose for me. I began talking to him daily, usually because I was mad at him for letting this pain stop me in what was supposed to be the prime of my life. Finally, in the lowest depths of pain and confusion, I called out to God and said, 'I get it. I can't do this. In fact, I don't know how long I can go on like this.'

In those moments, I began finding an odd sense of peace and faith. I could almost hear God saying to me, 'You will go on. I will hold you together when you feel like you are about to come undone. I will put you back together if you fall apart. I will do these things, not you.'

I believe that now. While I don't believe that pain itself is a blessing, it has created opportunities for me to seek out God. The pain made me stop, be still, and search for God. I don't believe I would have sought him out had I not been looking for answers to the "why" of my pain and suffering. It's possible that I would have continued living my life keeping God at arm's length, not accepting my need for him. I had so much pride in what I was able to accomplish and very little gratitude for all that God has done.

It's strange because I am so much more limited and yet much more grateful than I was before pain entered my life. Each physical set-back gives me an invitation to rely on God. I have the capacity to find joy in very simple things. It sounds cliché but I'm now able to witness many small victories in a day and be thankful for them. This shift in perspective has taken place over several years and is still a work in progress. There are still some days when despair wins the day. I am human. But through it all, God continues to reveal His presence in my life. He reminds me that every time I have felt alone in my experience and pain, he is always with me."

Chapter 4 – Journaling Questions

1. What are the things you wouldn't have if it weren't for your chronic illness or pain? Write out a list of what you have gained because physical suffering entered your life.

2. Read Ephesians 1:3-14. In these verses you will find a list of spiritual blessings available to those who know Christ. Unlike all that chronic pain has taken away from us, these are blessings that are available to us at any time and in any place.

   Write out a list of the blessings recorded in these verses.

   Journal your thoughts on how you have seen these blessings in your own life.

3. Meditate on these verses from the Psalms that speak of God as everything we need. Consider what God is saying to you through these verses. Journal or pray your response.

"I said to the Lord, 'You are my Lord; apart from you I have no good thing.'... Lord, *you alone are my portion and my cup*; you make my lot secure" (Psalm 16:2,5).

"The Lord is my Shepherd, *I lack nothing*" (Psalm 23:1).

"Whom have I in heaven but you? And *earth has nothing I desire besides you*. My flesh and my heart may fail, but God is the strength of my heart and my portion forever" (Psalm 73:25-26).

"I cry to you, LORD; I say, "You are my refuge, *my portion in the land of the living*" (Psalm 142:5).

CHAPTER 5

Our Sorrowful, Joyous Chronic Pain Life

Life with illness and pain is not all sorrow and grief. Our lives are filled with a deep suffering that can only be mourned, but there is more to this life than calling out to God in our distress.

I look at my friends who deal with unimaginable pain and challenging symptoms. Knowing all that goes on in their lives, I might expect to see constant weeping and sorrow. But I see so much more. I see resilience and laughter. I see normal conversations about food and books and movies and hobbies and ideas. I see people making horrible moments a little better for themselves and those around them.

All is not loss. For every family that leaves, I see another family who loves and supports and protects in the hardest of times. For every job that is lost, I see individuals finding ways to step out and make the world a better place, even as they suffer, even as they grieve. For every relapse and new diagnosis, I find those who are celebrating times of remission and days of relief. Between the tears, I see jokes and laughter thrown back and forth about the ridiculous things people say and the stranger-than-fiction medical professionals who, perhaps, shouldn't be practicing medicine.

We laugh so we don't cry. We joke because it makes the craziness of our lives more bearable. We find reasons to be happy because we know if we can't be happy while we are in pain, we will never be happy at all. And who wants to live a life like that? No one.

So we infuse our days with things that make us happy, we create moments of laughter, and we choose to experience joy when joy would not be the expected response. We are living proof of Proverbs 14:13 that "Even in laughter the heart may ache, and rejoicing may end in grief." This is our joyous, sorrowful chronic pain life. This is us finding joy in the pain. This is us believing we will find the goodness of the Lord in the land of the living. This is our rebellion – just because we are in pain doesn't mean we can't be happy.

As long as we have pain and illness, sorrow and mourning will remain. Grief will be a lifelong process because, for many, pain is a lifelong trial. Our goal is not to replace the sorrow and mourning with joy; rather, our sorrows comingle with our joys, as we mourn our losses and rejoice in our God simultaneously and together. We are following in the footsteps of Paul who lived his life as a sorrowful man who was always rejoicing (II Corinthians 6:10). We recognize the continued importance of grieving throughout our daily lives of pain, but this is not the end of our story or the fullness of what we strive for.

A glorious and inexpressible joy is available to those who know Christ. I imagine this joy as our capacity to experience the love and goodness of God. And it is because of the unceasing nature of God's love and goodness that joy is available to us regardless of our circumstances, regardless of what is going on in our bodies and in the world. God's promise to us is that we will see his goodness, even here, even now, in the land of the living. Joy is found when we look for his goodness, find his goodness, even as we suffer.

Joy in the Pain

I flash back to a moment. I am sitting at the table eating breakfast with my husband. Not eating breakfast lying down on the couch. Not hastily eating a bite so I can get back to lying down. Not eating breakfast in the other room on my own. No. Sitting at the kitchen table eating eggs and toast with my husband. Steaming hot cup of coffee in my hand. Pain levels, for the moment, controlled. Conversation. Feeling like a human being after months of constant flaring which left me barely able to leave the couch even for meals. The moment is surreal, an out of body experience as I indulge in the pleasure of sitting up to eat instead of lying down.

How do I describe this experience? How do I describe an experience that is so normal, so regular, but in the moment feels as though I am experiencing some intoxicating pleasure?

Like many other people with chronic pain, my pain levels ebb and flow, and there are times, magnificent times, when I break through to glorious places of decreased pain. Eating breakfast, I begin to experience levels of joy that appear completely unreasonable to the situation. I am practically giddy with delight. A huge grin is plastered on my face. The difference between normal pain levels and the pleasure of sitting at the table and experiencing a body that feels closer to normal is breathtaking, joy-inducing, and overwhelmingly sweet.

My friend and I were discussing this feeling of euphoria that sometimes comes when we are able to participate in normal life. She was having a low pain day and shared her excitement over feeling well enough to go to the grocery store. "My pain" she told me, "has given me the opportunity to celebrate just going to the grocery story. It brings me real joy. I feel good about it. I celebrate it. There aren't many people, except those who are ill, who are celebrating going to the store. I don't sit around in pain thinking '*Oh this is joyous!*' but when I do have these moments of joy, it is true joy. Intense joy."

Suffering makes the times of good so much sweeter. And I consider this from the perspective of eternity. I consider the joy set before us. That day when the tears will be wiped from my eyes, and I will know in my heart that death is no more. I am waiting for that day when I will no longer mourn, cry, or feel any pain. I am waiting for the former things to pass away, for that day when I get to *dwell with God.*

When I think of this glorious hope, I am reminded to not lose heart. I am reminded that, "Though outwardly we are wasting away, yet inwardly we are being renewed day by day. For our light and momentary troubles are achieving for us an eternal glory that far outweighs them all" (II Corinthians 4:16b-17). Can we even imagine the joy we will experience when we reach this eternal glory? Then will come a joyous day to begin everlasting joyous days.

Weeping and Wailing, Laughing and Singing

Until that day comes, we are learning to live a life of pain and illness in which our joys and our sorrows, our losses and our God-given gains intermingle in a way that is pleasing to God. We have so much hope and so much capacity to experience God's love and goodness here on earth, but we deeply feel the pain of loss as a burning longing within our souls for something better, something greater that is yet to come.

This intermingling of sorrow and joy is portrayed so beautifully in the book of Ezra, as the Israelites rebuild the foundation of the temple of the Lord. In this passage is captured a picture, a beautiful metaphor, of our joyous, sorrowful chronic pain life.

When the builders laid the foundation of the temple of the Lord, the priests in their vestments and with trumpets, and the Levites (the sons of Asaph) with cymbals, took their places to praise the Lord, as prescribed by David king of Israel. With praise and thanksgiving they sang to the Lord:

"He is good; his love toward Israel endures forever."

And all the people gave a great shout of praise to the Lord, because the foundation of the house of the Lord was laid. But many of the older priests and Levites and family heads, who had seen the former temple, wept aloud when they saw the foundation of the temple being laid, while many others shouted for joy. No one could distinguish the sound of the shouts of joy from the sound of weeping, because the people made so much noise. And the sound was heard far away (Ezra 3:10-13).

So much joy. And so much weeping. Both together and at the same time, one drowning out the other, mixing in such a way that they have become one and combined. There is much reason for sadness and much reason for joy. We are entering a time in the Israelite's history when they are rebuilding the sacred temple of the Lord, the house in which the Lord resides. It is an exciting time because a new foundation is being established in which the glory of the Lord will be held and realized.

But the older priests remember the glory of the old temple, the gold and silver, the fine cloth and exquisite materials. They remember the splendor of all the external features that made the temple beautiful and awe-inspiring. The temple that was once grand and magnificent now appears like nothing in comparison, and the older priests weep and wail for all that has been lost.

But something good is being done. The Lord has made a declaration: "'The glory of this present house will be greater than the glory of the former house,' says the Lord Almighty. 'And in this place I will grant peace,'" (Haggai 2:9). The Lord is declaring that though this house is lesser on the outside, it holds greater glory. It has been expanded, better equipped to house the glory of God in greater, more incredible ways.

History moves forward. Jesus lives, walks, dies, and is raised on this earth. He ascends into heaven, but leaves us the gift of the Holy

Spirit. And in this New Testament era, a new temple has been prepared. "Or do you not know that your body is a temple of the Holy Spirit?" (I Corinthians 6:19).

We are the temple; our bodies, humbly given to the Holy Spirit as his dwelling place. And in many ways, in the throes of chronic pain, God is doing a similar work as when he allowed the destruction and then rebuilding of the Old Testament temple. He breaks and rebuilds us so his glory in our lives shines brighter.

Chronic pain may have made us uglier in the physical. It may have made us feel less presentable. But our capacity to honor God in this new body far exceeds the old. Chronic pain is helping us put sin to death. It is helping us recognize the small goods around us, that we may praise God for all he has given. Chronic pain has made us smaller and God bigger. We are less consumed with our own praise and more driven to praise the God who made and sustains us.

We weep because the glory of our former physical body has passed away. Yet joy comes when we see how God is giving us more of himself than we ever had before. Joy comes when we realize we have been sanctified in ways that are eternal. And this is why we weep and mourn and wail, yet still laugh and dance and sing. We have lost so much, yet we have gained even more. And in our own lives, the mingling of our weeping and our shouts of joy is displayed to the world.

Chapter 5 Journaling Questions

1. How has chronic pain increased your capacity to experience joy over the small gifts God gives? For my friend, it was going to the grocery store. For me, it was through enjoying good food and conversation. Write out a list of the small moments when you have felt joy of this kind.

2. Read Psalm 27 and consider where you have seen God's goodness displayed in your life. Write out a list of how his goodness and love have been apparent, even as you suffer and experience pain.

3. Paul described himself as a sorrowful man who was always rejoicing (II Corinthians 6:10). What would it look like to live this out in your own life?

End Notes

1. Gaskin, D. J., & Richard, P. (2011). The economic costs of pain in the United States. *The Journal of Pain, 13*(8), 715-724.

2. Breivik, H., Collett, B., Ventafridda, V., Cohen, R., & Gallacher, D. (2006). Survey of chronic pain in Europe: Prevalence, impact on daily life, and treatment. *European Journal of Pain Management, 10*(4), 287-333.

3. Glantz, M. J., Chamberlain, M. C., Liu, Q., Hsieh, C., Edwards, K., Van Horn, A., & Recht, L. (2009). Gender disparity in the rate of partner abandonment in patients with serious medical illness. *Cancer, 115*(22), 5237-5242.

4. Tozer, A. W. (2011). *The Pursuit of God.* Harrisburg, PA: Christian Publications Inc.

More From the Chronic Pain and the Christian Life Series

But God, Wouldn't I Be More Useful to You if I Were Healthy?